KV-370-325

WHAT'S AT ISSUE?

DRUGS & YOU

Bridget Lawless

Heinemann
LIBRARY

www.heinemann.co.uk
Visit our website to find out more information about **Heinemann Library** books.

To order:
☎ Phone 44 (0) 1865 888066
 Send a fax to 44 (0) 1865 314091
 Visit the Heinemann Bookshop at www.heinemann.co.uk to browse our catalogue and order online.

First published in Great Britain by Heinemann Library, Halley Court, Jordan Hill, Oxford OX2 8EJ, a division of Reed Educational and Professional Publishing Ltd.
Heinemann is a registered trademark of Reed Educational & Professional Publishing Limited.

OXFORD MELBOURNE AUCKLAND
JOHANNESBURG BLANTYRE GABORONE
IBADAN PORTSMOUTH NH (USA) CHICAGO

Designed by Tinstar Design (www.tinstar.co.uk)
Illustrations by Oxford Illustrators and Jeff Edwards
Originated by Ambassador Litho Ltd
Printed by Wing King Tong in Hong Kong

ISBN 0 431 03530 X (hardback)   ISBN 0 431 03535 0 (paperback)
04 03 02 01 00   04 03 02 01 00
10 9 8 7 6 5 4 3 2   10 9 8 7 6 5 4 3 2 1

British Library Cataloguing in Publication Data

Lawless, Bridget
        Drugs and you. – (What's at issue)
        1. Drug abuse – Juvenile literature 2. Teenagers – Drug use –
        Juvenile literature
        I. Title
        362.2'9

Acknowledgements

The Publishers would like to thank the following for permission to reproduce photographs:
The Advertising Archives p 38; Bubbles/Jennie Woodcock p 16; Trevor Clifford p 42; Corbis p 15, 33/ Richard Bickel, p 14/Jacques Chenet p 37/Francois de Mulder p32; Liz Eddison pp 27, 30; Mary Evans Picture Library p 6; Health Education Authority pp 18, 19; Parachute Pictures/David Browne p 13, 20, 21(t); Photofusion/Warren Powell p 22/Stuart Sanders p 4/David Tothill p 39; Popperfoto/Oliver Morin p 34; Rex Features pp 10, 12, 31, 41; The Stockmarket/imaggio/Kalish p 28; Tony Stone Images/Peter Dokus p 5/Lori Adamski Peek p 43; Science Photo Library p 24/Connor Caffrey, p 9/Adam Hart-Davis, p25 / Cordelia Molloy p 21(b)/Hank Morgan p 11/James Prince p 8/Sinclair Stammers p 23/Sheila Terry p 26.

Cover photograph reproduced with permission of Trevor Clifford Photography

Our thanks to Julie Turner (School Counsellor, Banbury School, Oxfordshire) for her comments in the preparation of this book.

Every effort has been made to contact copyright holders of any material reproduced in this book. Any omissions will be rectified in subsequent printings if notice is given to the Publisher.

Any words appearing in the text in bold, **like this**, are explained in the Glossary.

Contents

Introduction

There are many widely opposing views about drugs and the people who use them. Some people feel that drugs are a means of escaping reality, part of an alternative lifestyle and a way of exploring the possibilities of body or mind. Others claim that drugs are evil, destructive, a menace to society and the cause of crime, misery, addiction and death. Some insist that drugs are harmless fun, a way of relaxing and an important creative influence behind many of our greatest artists, writers and musicians. Each of these conflicting opinions is true in a way – which is why drugs spark such heated debates about personal freedom, social responsibility and which drugs should or should not be legal. This book will help you explore this complex subject and show that where drugs are concerned, nobody has all the answers.

What are drugs?

The search for a '**high**' leads some to a lifetime of serious drug abuse. This heroin addict is injecting.

When people think of drugs, usually a negative image comes into their mind – perhaps a much publicized death, a gloomy poster warning of the dangers or a desperate person injecting themselves in a grubby room. But drugs play a much wider part in our lives, and some have positive, healing effects, saving or improving rather than ruining lives.

The term 'drugs' covers a wide range of substances that can affect the physical or mental state. They include illegal or **controlled drugs** such as heroin, cocaine, cannabis and ecstasy; **prescribed** medicines obtained from a chemist or hospital; medicines bought **over-the-counter**, such as aspirin and paracetamol; and legal drugs such as the **caffeine** found in tea and coffee, the **nicotine** in tobacco and of course, alcohol.

Illegal or controlled drugs

Controlled or 'illegal' drugs are governed by laws about their possession and supply. They include some preparations meant for medicinal use. Others are naturally occurring plant substances, either in their raw state or prepared for use in ways that help get the drug quickly into the bloodstream. Some controlled drugs are chemically **synthetic** – they mimic the **mind-altering** properties of certain naturally occurring chemicals and plants, such as opium and cannabis, or are new creations invented in the laboratory.

Legal drugs

Most drugs that we term 'legal' are not controlled by laws at all, or they just have restrictions on the age at which someone can buy them or use them in public. For example, you can drink alcohol at any age, but you cannot buy or drink alcohol in a pub until you are 18 years old. You can smoke cigarettes at any age, but legally you cannot buy tobacco until you are aged 16. Caffeine, a **stimulant** found in tea, coffee and cola, can be used freely by children and adults alike.

Glue-sniffing, solvents and volatile substances

Household products which give off vapours that can be inhaled, such as glue, lighter gas and aerosols, are often included under the term 'drugs'. In fact, these are not drugs but **solvents**, or **volatile** substances. Volatile-substance abuse, or VSA, describes the misuse of these products for their drug-like effects.

Misuse and abuse – defining the terms

The terms 'misuse' and 'abuse' are often used in relation to drugs. Unfortunately the words themselves are frequently misused and their meanings muddled! Drug misuse means using something for a different purpose than normally intended. Some people misuse medicines to get '**high**'. Drug abuse means the wrong or unwise use of a drug or substance with drug-like properties. It suggests a harmful outcome, so drinking a damaging amount of alcohol is alcohol abuse and taking a damaging amount of drugs is drug abuse.

EFFECTS OF DRUGS

Stimulants (caffeine, amphetamines, cocaine, ecstasy) wake you up, excite you or make you more alert.
Depressants (**tranquillizers**, alcohol) calm you down, lower your spirits or sedate you.
Opiates (opium) and **narcotics** (heroin) relieve pain, calm you and make you sleep.
Hallucinogens (LSD, magic mushrooms) cause hallucinations so that you see or imagine things that are not real.

Alcohol and tobacco are drugs that adults can use freely. However, both carry serious health risks and can result in **addiction**.

A brief history of drugs

Drugs have been in almost every society since ancient times. Many plants have properties that affect the body or alter **perception** and people have always eaten, drunk or smoked these substances for pleasure, or as part of their **rituals**. The process of **fermentation** which produces alcohol was discovered many thousands of years ago, enabling **intoxicating** drinks to be made from ordinary plants, fruits and vegetables.

No doubt, throughout history, there have always been some people who have misused whatever drugs were available and caused problems for themselves and society. Drugs have also been deliberately used by many powers to weaken the population of the countries they want to control.

The Opium Wars

In the 18th century, Britain supported the powerful East India Company, which imported vast amounts of Indian opium into China. Millions of Chinese people became **addicts**. When the Chinese government objected to this weakening of its population, Britain fought to protect its profitable opium trade. China was defeated in the resulting Opium Wars and had to surrender to British interests.

Addictive pain-killers

In the 19th century, **morphine** (an opium-based pain-killer) was widely used in the American Civil War. The drug's calming effects also helped block out the horrors that soldiers witnessed. Many returned home addicted to morphine for

life. Other opium remedies such as **laudanum** were, by then, being sold in England and America. No one in respectable society would have admitted they had a drug problem, yet thousands were secretly addicted to these opium remedies.

This engraving, for a journal published in 1891, shows morphine addiction amongst women in 'respectable society'.

INJECTING DRUGS

The invention of the **hypodermic** needle, or syringe, in the 19th century meant drugs could be injected straight into the bloodstream. This brought on the effects much more quickly.

The birth of the modern 'drug scene'

The 20th century has probably seen the greatest variety of drugs in use across the world. Many new drugs have been invented in the laboratory and household products have increased the number of ways people have found to get **high**. From the 1920s to the 1950s each generation had its favoured drugs – cannabis, heroin, amphetamines or cocaine. Gradually, a separate subculture emerged, where drug use, music and creativity were closely linked.

The psychedelic experience

Drug-taking became far more widespread among young people during the hippy movement of the 1960s and 1970s. It was part of this 'alternative' subculture. Cannabis became very popular and the **hallucinogenic** drug LSD was widely in use. The drug-induced 'psychedelic experience' of wild colour, patterns and sounds influenced fashions, art and music worldwide.

The distinctive cannabis leaf became a symbol of peaceful drug-use in the 1970s.

Don't do what I do, do what I say…

Drugs have been in mainstream society for more than a generation. Thousands of parents, politicians and leaders have themselves experimented with **controlled** substances. Now that they are in positions of responsibility, they feel obliged to discourage and condemn illegal drug use. More often than not public figures feel it is wise to deny their own experiences.

CREATIVE INFLUENCE

Thousands of famous artists, musicians, writers and philosophers have used drugs for inspiration. Examples include Thomas De Quincey and Samuel Coleridge from the 19th century, and Pablo Picasso and Jack Kerouac from the 20th century. Some people claim that artificially **altered perception** has been responsible for many steps in human creative development.

Who takes drugs today?

Although the term 'drug user' often suggests the image of a thin, sunken-eyed young person injecting heroin, drugs are actually used by all kinds of people, of all classes, ages and races. Drugs are used in towns, cities and rural areas all over the world. In fact, the vast majority of people in the world who have access to some kind of drug, including alcohol, tobacco and caffeine, take at least one of them.

Starting young

Young people may start experimenting with drugs in their teens and early twenties, but in the developed world they are trying drugs at an even earlier age. A small proportion go on to have a serious drug problem all their lives. The majority lose interest in illegal drugs in their twenties.

Why do people take drugs?

There are many different reasons why people experiment with drugs, and many reasons why they choose to continue taking them, or to stop. The first attraction is usually that they have heard that drugs are fun. Friends or older people may talk about the pleasurable effects of getting **high** or 'out if it'. The risks may seem remote, or they may even add to the attraction.

Cannabis is the most widely used illegal drug. Many early cannabis users continue to smoke it occasionally for the rest of their lives.

People often talk about peer group pressure – feeling forced to do something just to fit in – as a reason for people taking drugs. But equally often, young people just have a natural curiosity, want to share ideas as they form social groups and make decisions about their own lives. Rebellion against adult values may also play a part, and the illicit nature of drug use can be an added attraction. Leaving home for college or university may give new opportunities to try the 'forbidden' away from parents' eyes.

FACTS

● *28% of the UK population admit having used illegal drugs at least once.*
● *5% of 12–13 year-olds, 13% of 13–14 year-olds, 25% of 14–15 year-olds and 24% of 16–29 year-olds admit taking* **controlled drugs** *in the last year.*

Drugs can be a means of escape

Living in depressing surroundings without much hope for the future, feeling helpless and lost or unloved are all factors that can make someone reach for a drink or drug that will block reality out. It might bring some pleasure, but it's not being done for fun. Some experts say that using drugs is self-destructive, but for some people it may feel like a means of survival.

Part of the social scene

Many drugs become part of a particular social setting. Ecstasy, taken by millions of young people every weekend, is almost exclusively used in the dance scene. Cocaine, once known as the champagne drug, has become associated with the music, film and professional worlds. Its more dangerous and **addictive** relative, crack, has no such glamorous associations. Crack tends to be associated with criminal

activity – theft, **prostitution** and drug dealing. Heroin, with its reputation as the **addicts'** drug, has increasingly been used as a prop by stressed professionals. Steroids, once only abused by body-builders and athletes, are now widely in use in clubs and bars. Steroid users are said to be the fastest growing group of drug addicts in Britain.

Drugs may give temporary relief from problems, but giving them up gets harder every time they are taken. This user has collapsed after taking heroin.

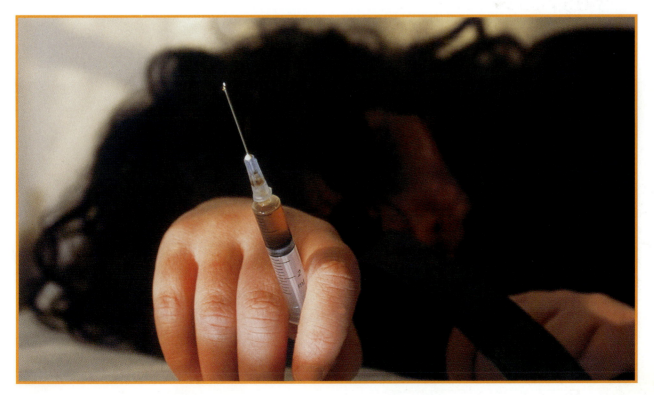

Health risks (1)

Psychological and physical harm

From the outside using drugs can look like fun. However, there are serious **psychological** and physical dangers that mean any kind of drug-taking is a risk.

What are the risks?

Drugs can kill, do permanent physical or mental damage or have terrible long-term effects on a person's general state of health. Most drug users have no real concept of the dangers and take the most extraordinary risks to get **high**. Most drugs come from unknown sources, are of unknown purity and are delivered in unknown doses. This means that drug users cannot be sure what a substance really is, and so cannot assess the risks they are taking.

Drugs are different for everyone

Just as some people can 'hold their drink' and others cannot, a real danger with drugs is that different people react very differently to the same substances. A drug that has no apparent harmful effect on nine people can kill the tenth. Anyone can have an unexpected physical reaction to a drug, even a drug they have taken many times before. That risk is much higher if the person has an unknown heart condition or **allergy**, or has also taken other drugs, alcohol or medication.

Surroundings and mood

The effect of a drug can be influenced by the surroundings it is taken in and the mood the person is already in. With **hallucinogenic** drugs like LSD, a 'bad trip' can last 12 terrifying hours or more, and the psychological damage affects some people permanently.

How much are you taking?

Because sources and production methods vary, the quality and strength of illegal drugs varies. Unexpectedly pure batches of powerful drugs like heroin frequently kill unsuspecting users. However, drugs are more often bulked out or **cut** with cheaper drugs and other substances, making them more profitable for the **dealer**. These bulking agents may be toxic in themselves – imagine sniffing

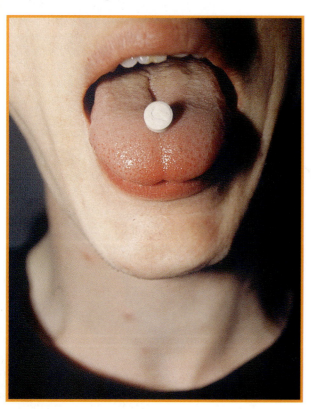

This drug user is about to swallow an ecstasy tablet and knows nothing of the dangerous impurities it may contain.

scouring powder, for example, or injecting brick dust, as thousands of heroin users do, leaving terrible infections that refuse to heal.

With drugs in your system…

After taking a drug, you don't know what you might do. The influence of a drug can lead to injury or death indirectly – by affecting your actions or your judgement so that you take harmful or fatal risks. Sometimes passing out saves someone from doing themselves further harm, although if they are sick there is a real risk of choking to death on their own vomit.

Damaging the body

When drug taking becomes a regular habit, the body and mind are being constantly interfered with. The unnatural extremes of highs followed by lows can result in depression, anxiety, **paranoia** and nervousness. Eating and sleeping patterns are disturbed. Exhaustion can then cause other risks because judgement and concentration are affected. Long-term drug use can also damage the heart, lungs, liver or kidneys and may cause **infertility**.

FACTS

- *An increasing number of road accidents are caused by drivers under the influence of drugs.*
- *Young people are more likely to have unsafe sex if they have been drinking or taking drugs. They risk sexually transmitted disease, HIV infection and unwanted pregnancy.*

Every year thousands of young people end up in hospital after a bad experience with drugs or alcohol.

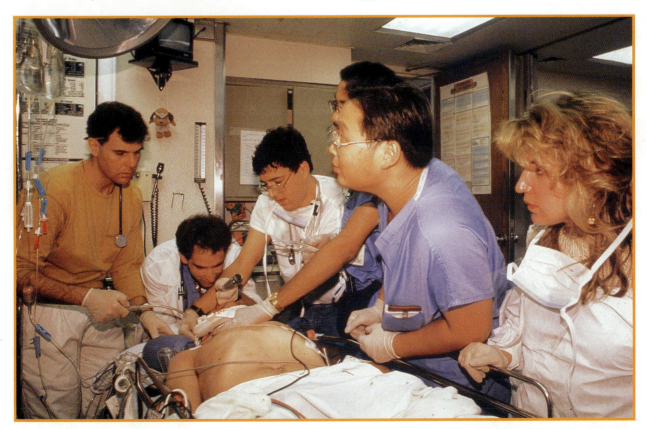

Health risks (2)

Injecting

Despite the many dangers associated with injecting, more and more people are injecting drugs today. This not only includes the traditionally injected substances such as morphine and heroin, but increasingly amphetamines, barbiturates and drug mixtures or 'cocktails', too. All these are shot directly into the blood stream via a needle.

Injecting is by far the riskiest way of getting drugs into the body. Infections such as **HIV** and **hepatitis**, which are carried in the blood, are easily spread by needle-sharing. Dirty needles can also lead to **abscesses** or **septicaemia**, blood poisoning. Repeated injecting into veins can make them collapse, so that a new vein must be used. Collapsed veins cut off the blood supply, eventually killing the limb. Every year hundreds of drug injectors develop **gangrene** – their arm, leg or foot rots away and then has to be amputated.

Addiction

Another major concern about drugs is the powerful physical or **psychological** need called addiction. A drug **addict** suffers a desperate, uncontrollable craving and feels deeply anxious or physically ill without the drug. They can think of nothing except where the next 'hit' will come from and will do almost anything to get it. Once they have taken the drug, the bad feelings disappear, but only until they need the next fix.

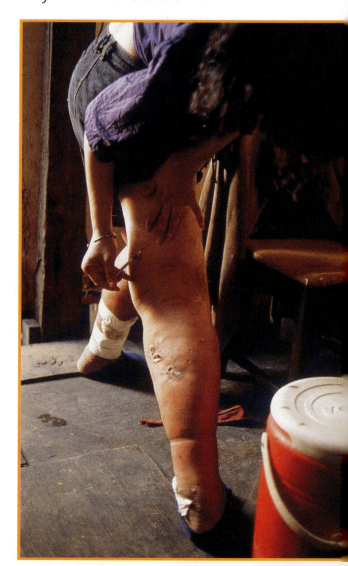

FACTS

More than 20,000 people sought help for drug problems at UK agencies in 1997:
- *12.5% were under 20 years old*
- *there were 3 times as many males as females*
- *heroin was being used by over 50%*
- *65% had injected drugs at some time.*

If a limb suffers from blocked veins or infections that will not heal it may have to be amputated.

Some drugs are extremely **addictive**, others not at all. Crack is probably the most addictive substance in the world, but heroin and even its medically approved substitute methadone, create millions of addicts worldwide every year. Coming off a drug when you are addicted (sometimes called 'cold turkey') is a long, agonizing process with very unpleasant physical and emotional side effects. With medical support the process can be more easily managed – but it is still tough.

The experience is so hard that many long-term users try repeatedly to 'kick the habit' without success. The downward spiral back into drug use is often made worse by the sense of failure, making the calming effects of the drug the person has tried to quit seem all the more welcome. Watching someone go through the process can be heartbreaking. Some parents get drugs for their addicted

Getting addicted is easy – but it can be a long, lonely journey getting your life back in control again. These addicts in Thailand have been given herbal medicine to make them vomit and cleanse their bodies of addictive drugs.

children because they cannot bear to see them suffering. Others turn them over to the police in the hope that the law can break the cycle.

KICKING THE HABIT

The phrase 'kicking the habit' came about because of the involuntary leg-jerking that happens when a regular user tries to come off heroin.

COLD TURKEY

During another phase of the process, the person feels cold and shivers uncontrollably, making goose-pimples that look like turkey skin.

Social harm

Damaging relationships

The social problems caused by taking drugs can be just as damaging as the physical risks. The most obvious problem is that drugs can change the way a person behaves so that their relationships with other people may suffer. They may reject a more stable group of friends to spend time with other drug users. They are likely to conceal their habit from disapproving friends, their family, teachers or employer. Their dealings with other people may generally become secretive, dishonest and irresponsible. Someone in a deep relationship with drugs is rarely able to care properly for others and has to put his or her own needs first. A serious drug user cannot cope with being challenged – they may become abusive, threatening or physically violent if they cannot get what they want.

Getting money for drugs

Drugs cost money but tend to reduce the ability to earn it. Even small-scale drug use by a young person can cost more money than they have. A drug user's need for money can make them behave in ways they would not have dreamt of before drugs were in the picture. Selling personal belongings is often the first step and when there is nothing of their own left to sell they may sell other people's possessions, or start to steal from their friends or family. Obviously, if they are found out the victims are likely to feel very angry and betrayed, and close relationships are again damaged. Stealing from cars, houses or shops may be the

Drugs have a high price for many young people who end up selling sex to pay for their habit.

next step, possibly leading to violent robbery or mugging. Credit card fraud is another favourite way of funding drug use. Selling drugs may be an easy option but for many selling sex becomes an increasingly attractive means of raising quick cash.

School exclusions

There are other serious kinds of social harm associated with problem drug use. A student involved with drugs at school or college faces very heavy penalties if they are caught, including being permanently **excluded** from school. They could be throwing away the chance of an education because finding another school may not be easy. How many head teachers are likely to welcome a known drug user and perhaps invite drug problems into their schools?

Loss of employment

Losing a job because of drug or alcohol abuse is a similar problem. Often, the issue comes to light because the person can no longer cope with their work. A private weakness suddenly becomes public when someone is dismissed or has to declare to a potential new employer that they have drug charges against their name.

Getting a reputation

Some people enjoy the reputation of being associated with drugs. They think it makes them seem streetwise or cool. However, someone who boasts about drugs in a playground or pub can soon become someone everyone thinks is a 'dope-head', feels sorry for, or avoids because they are always after money for drugs.

Being stoned, drunk or **high** rarely looks so cool from the outside.

Legal risks

As well as health risks and social problems, getting involved with drugs can also lead to legal trouble – which can seriously affect a person's freedom and future prospects. Anyone using **controlled drugs** risks being caught by the police and charged. **Dealers** face heavier legal penalties, even if they are only selling enough to pay for their own drug use. Wholesale suppliers and **traffickers** face the toughest sentences of all.

Possession

In most countries, the **possession** of controlled drugs and some medicines, unless **prescribed**, is illegal. Where soft drugs like cannabis are involved, if a person arrested for possession admits their guilt the police might offer a **caution** – a kind of verbal warning – instead of charging them. This helps prevent the courts from getting clogged up with thousands of minor drug offences. However, a caution is still serious. A record is kept of the crime and it will be taken into account as a previous offence if the person is caught again. A caution might also require the offender to attend a course or drug advisory centre to help him or her work towards a change of behaviour.

If a person found with a drug denies possession, the police may decide to **prosecute**. If found guilty the person will face **probation**, fines or a prison sentence, and get a criminal record.

> ### FACT
>
> *Almost 90% of the drug offences that reach the UK courts are for possession of cannabis.*

A young person can be prosecuted from the age of legal responsibility, which in the UK is ten years old. These youths are entering a Magistrates Court to face charges for drug offences.

MAXIMUM SENTENCES

In the UK drugs are mainly covered by the Misuse of Drugs Act and the Medicines Act. They divide drugs into groups depending on how dangerous or addictive they are considered to be. Sentencing for offences is determined by the class of the drug and the previous convictions of the offender.

	Possession	Supply
Class A	7 years prison	life
Class B	5 years prison	14 years
Class C	2 years	5 years

Class A: heroin, cocaine, crack, ecstasy, LSD, methadone, opium, magic mushrooms dried for use, also any Class B drugs (see below) that have been prepared into a form for injection

Class B: cannabis, amphetamine, barbiturates

Class C: benzodiazapine tranquillizers (e.g. Temazepam), mild amphetamines

Dealing and trafficking

Supplying drugs, or 'dealing', is always considered more serious than possession. Depending on the class of the drug concerned, a dealer found guilty faces higher fines, and is much more likely to get a prison sentence. Dealing and drug trafficking may result in life imprisonment. The offender's house, car and any other assets thought to be from the proceeds of supplying drugs can be taken away.

Getting a criminal record

A person with a record for a drug offence (even if only cautioned) is marked as a law-breaker and gains the reputation of being a criminal. Even when a caution has expired or a sentence has been completed, the offence usually remains on record in some form or other. Years later, perhaps long after a youthful brush with the law, the person could still be prevented from applying for certain kinds of training or work. They may be regarded as unsuitable for positions of responsibility and refused entry to certain countries.

Coming to police notice

Anyone who hangs around with known drug users or dealers runs the risk of coming to police notice. In the course of their daily duty, officers keep a sharp eye on who knows who and what faces are seen in those places associated with drugs or other crimes. This information is gathered as 'intelligence' – a way of putting a picture together so that criminals can be identified and crimes prevented or solved.

Police forces keep computer records of people seen in the company of known drug users and dealers.

17

Controlled drugs (1)

Controlled drugs are medicinal and non-medicinal drugs, the use of which is governed by laws about **possession** and supply.

Amphetamines

Type of drug: **stimulant**
Other names: speed, uppers, whiz, pep pills and many others
Legal status: Class B or Class A if prepared for injection. It is illegal to possess amphetamine without a prescription.

Amphetamines were first made in the 1930s as a treatment for asthma. They were given to soldiers during several wars, from World War II through to the Vietnam War, to keep them alert when they had little sleep. They were also **prescribed** as slimming pills, until doctors realized that more people were taking them for pleasure than as a dieting aid. Today they are rarely prescribed and most amphetamines are made illegally for the drug market.

Amphetamine increases **adrenaline** production in the body, making the user more energetic, alert and confident. It enables them to stay up dancing, partying or working all night. It also suppresses the appetite. When it wears off feelings of tiredness and depression take over. If taken regularly, the user may become very run down, aggressive, **paranoid** and unable to sleep.

Amphetamine is sniffed, swallowed, injected or rubbed on the gums.

Amyl nitrites

Type of drug: stimulant
Other names: poppers, liquid gold, rush
Legal status: These have been manufactured and sold legally as a 'room deodorizer' but if supplied as a mood-altering drug they are classed as a medicine and are illegal unless under prescription.

Amyl nitrite is a clear or golden liquid and usually comes in a small bottle. Its vapours are sniffed, causing dizziness and a **high** lasting just a few minutes. It is often used by dancers in nightclubs to give them a quick boost. It relaxes the muscles and can increase sexual pleasure.

Sniffing poppers produces a brief rush.

Cannabis

Type of drug: affects people in different ways so cannot be classed as a **depressant** or stimulant

Other names: general – dope, blow, pot, draw; herbal form – grass, herb hemp, marijuana, weed; resin form – oil, hash and others; cannabis cigarettes – spliff, joints, reefers

Legal status: Class B. It is illegal to supply, possess, or grow cannabis or to allow its use on your premises.

Cannabis can be smoked in specially rolled cigarettes, baked in cakes, eaten raw or drunk as a tea. It creates a relaxed state of **altered perception** known as being 'stoned'. This can be a talkative or inward-looking mood, or may be a very creative frame of mind. Cannabis can make a group of users laugh a lot. A sudden hunger often felt after taking cannabis is known as the 'munchies'.

Cannabis can affect motivation so that a person may be less able or driven to do

Cannabis is said by many to have important medical uses. Official researchers are developing a pure strain which may one day be prescribed to relieve conditions such as cancer, multiple sclerosis and **AIDS**.

things, but have the feeling that they are capable of anything and full of great ideas. It makes some people feel extremely sick and stronger types of cannabis can cause paranoia or **hallucination**. Cannabis is by far the most widely used controlled drug and the subject of much debate. Many people believe it is not harmful and that using it should not be a crime.

GANJA

Used by people for thousands of years, cannabis plays an important part in many religions and cultures. **Rastafarians** (members of a West Indian religious and political sect) call cannabis *ganja* and believe it gives them spiritual powers.

Controlled drugs (2)

Cocaine

Type of drug: **stimulant**
Other names: coke, Charlie, C, snort, toot, snow
Legal status: Class A

Cocaine is derived from the leaves of the coca tree which grows in South America. For thousands of years, people from this region have chewed the leaves to get a feeling of well-being and to help them endure hard work in high altitudes. Cocaine's **anaesthetic** properties were discovered in the 19th century. Dentists still use a form of it today when they numb the mouth with a local injection.

Illegally sold cocaine is a white powder, often **cut** with other similar looking

Doses of cocaine have to be repeated in 'runs' over several hours to maintain the effects. Sniffing cocaine in this way may cause damage to the tissues on the inside of the nose. Even the tissue that separates the nostrils can be destroyed.

products. It can be sniffed, put on the tongue, injected or smoked. The most common way of taking it is by making little lines of cocaine on a shiny surface and sniffing them up through a rolled banknote or straw. The drug quickly enters the bloodstream and the user feels a surge of energy. Alertness, confidence and restless feelings follow. The effects only last half an hour and doses have to be taken regularly over several hours to maintain the **high**. Afterwards the user is likely to feel tired and depressed. The bad effects often get worse over time.

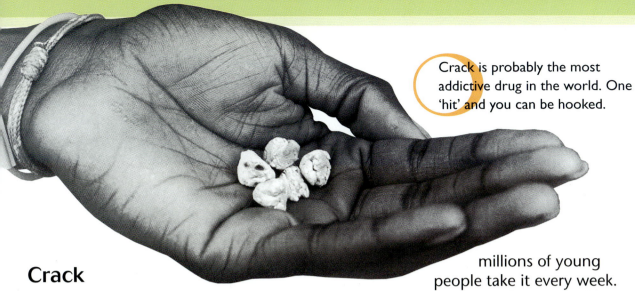

Crack is probably the most addictive drug in the world. One 'hit' and you can be hooked.

Crack

Type of drug: stimulant
Other names: base, freebase, rock, stone
Legal status: Class A

Crack is produced from cocaine and is sometimes called 'the cocaine fast-food'. It takes effect more quickly, but lasts an even shorter time than cocaine. Crack is extremely **addictive**. The small white crystal lumps or 'rocks' can be rolled with tobacco in a cigarette, heated so the smoke can be inhaled, or melted in water and injected. The **rush** is intense but the lows are lower. Crack is a huge problem in some American states and increasingly in other cities around the world. Its addictive nature means that wherever the use of crack is high, crime is always a major problem.

Ecstasy

Type of drug: stimulant and **hallucinogen**
Other names: E, love doves, M25s, and many others
Legal status: Class A

Ecstasy is an amphetamine with some hallucinogenic properties. It is widely associated with the dance scene and millions of young people take it every week. Taken as small pills or capsules, ecstasy raises energy levels and makes the user feel happy and loving towards others. If they are dancing, it is vital that they drink water regularly because the body **dehydrates** and gets dangerously hot, which can cause fatal blood clots. When the effects wear off, the user may feel anxious or **paranoid** and not be able to sleep. Ecstasy can kill, even when taken for the first time. As a relatively new drug in popular use, its long-term effects are not yet certain, but recent studies show alarming signs of permanent brain damage among users.

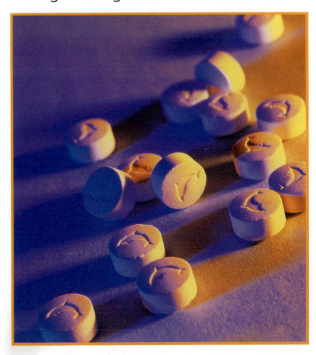

Brain damage may be the price paid by many of the millions who take ecstasy every week.

21

Controlled drugs (3)

Heroin

Type of drug: **opiate**
Other names: junk, H, horse, skag, smack.
Legal status: Class A

Heroin is one of a number of drugs derived from opium, a natural substance that comes from some types of poppy. Medically, heroin is used to relieve pain, particularly in cancer patients and the terminally ill. It was developed as a replacement to morphine, which is also made from opium. Hundreds of thousands of people became addicted to morphine in the 19th century. In the 20th century millions more have become addicted to heroin.

Most illegally produced heroin is made from opium that has been smuggled from the poppy-producing countries, such as India, Thailand and Turkey. Regular users quickly develop a tolerance to the drug, needing larger doses more often to achieve the same effects. Eventually, they need the drug just to prevent the unbearable feelings associated with withdrawal.

Methadone

Type of drug: similar to an opiate
Legal status: prescription only

Methadone is a **synthetic** drug, developed to mimic opium as a war-time pain-killer. Its effects are similar to opium. Today it is used to help heroin and morphine **addicts** withdraw from their drugs, but unfortunately many of these people have become addicted to methadone instead.

Heroin powder is often melted and injected, or can be smoked or sniffed. Heroin addicts run the risk of infections and blood diseases from dirty syringes, and from deep coma or death in the case of an overdose.

Anyone **prescribed** methadone has to collect their daily dose from the chemist and take it while still on the premises. To help prevent abuse, the liquid is made too sticky to inject.

People who take 'acid' never know the strength or likely outcome of the trip they will take.

LSD

Type of drug: **hallucinogen**
Other names: lysergic acid diethylamide, acid, trips, tabs
Legal status: Class A

LSD is a powerful synthetic non-addictive hallucinogen that first became popular in the 1970s. It is produced illegally as a white crystal powder and made into pills or capsules. Sometimes LSD drops are put on squares of paper printed with an image. The effects, which can last up to twelve hours, can be an extreme mixture of feelings, visions and inspiration that the user cannot control. A bad experience on LSD can be terrifying and is difficult to stop, even in an emergency. Unsurprisingly, some people who have taken LSD suffer serious **psychological** damage.

Magic mushrooms

Type of drug: hallucinogen
Other names: liberty cap, mushies
Legal status: unrestricted unless 'prepared for use'. The active ingredient psilocybin is a Class A drug.

Liberty caps are tiny brown mushrooms with a distinctive bump on top. They grow naturally in fields in autumn. Eaten or taken as a tea, the **hallucinogenic** effects are like a weaker version of LSD. Many would-be users find the mushroom make them feel sick. Identifying the right kind of mushroom can also be a problem as they look like many other small, brown mushrooms or toadstools that grow in grass. **Allergic** reactions to other species taken by mistake are also quite common. Because they grow freely in fields, parks and even gardens, the **possession** of magic mushrooms is difficult to control.

Controlled drugs and solvents (4)

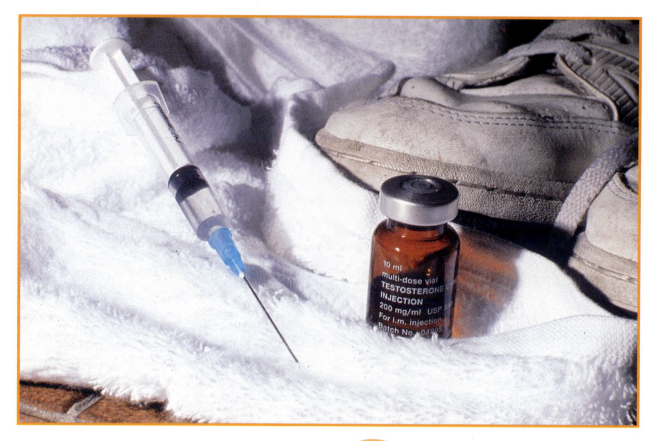

Steroids

Type of drug: **stimulant**
Other names: anabolic steroids, Stromba, Dianabol, Winstrol, Deca, roids, gear, juice
Legal status: Class C

Steroids are **hormones** and natural stimulants. They are used by body-builders and sportsmen and women because they help build their muscles and improve their physique. However, they are not only found in gyms and training centres. Increasingly, they are used by young people to improve their general

Taking steroids can permanently change the sexual characteristics of both men and women.

appearance and as general stimulant drugs.

The male hormone **testosterone** increases aggression and can turn a peaceful person violent. Male users may develop breasts, lose their sexual drive and become sterile. Women's periods may stop and they may develop deeper voices, smaller breasts, facial hair and enlarged sex organs. Both sexes often develop severe acne.

Tranquillizers

Type of drug: **depressant**
Other names: benzodiazepines,
barbiturates, tranx, eggs, jellies, downers,
Valium, Temazepam
Legal status: Class C if illegally supplied

Tranquillizers are a group of medicinal
drugs that are prescribed for stress and
anxiety, or in heavier doses as sleeping
pills. They calm tension and make the user
feel good, but often cause drowsiness and
an unsteadiness. Tranquillizers are very
addictive and there has been a worrying
history of doctors continuing to **prescribe**
them to patients for many years.

Most illegally sold tranquillizers are
obtained from prescriptions, the **dealer**
often registering with a number of
doctors. Taken in larger doses or mixed
with alcohol, they cause a feeling of well-
being or an effect similar to being drunk,
although mixing these two depressant
drugs can be fatal. Heroin **addicts**
sometimes inject tranquillizers when their
usual supplies of heroin dry up.

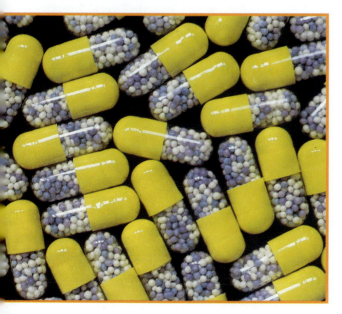

Solvents

Other names: glue, gas, aerosols, lighter
fluid, butane, **volatile** substances
Legal status: **possession** is not illegal, but
it is against the law to sell these products
to anyone under 18 if it is thought they
may intend to inhale them

Solvents are volatile substances with
vapours that have drug-like effects if
inhaled. They are not drugs but are often
familiar household products such as glues
and lighter fluid. These substances are
depressants. They are sniffed straight
from the container, or glue is put in a
plastic bag or crisps packet and the
vapours are inhaled. The user feels drunk
and dizzy. They may laugh a lot and feel
very relaxed or sleepy, or they may feel
sick and become unconscious. The effects
last about half-an-hour unless topped up.

Although the deaths rarely reach the
headlines, volatile **substance abuse** kills
more young people than any other drug.
Users sometimes put the plastic bag over
their head to give a constant supply of
the vapours, risking suffocation. Their
breathing may fail or their heart may
stop. If sick and unconscious, the person
may choke on their vomit.

FACTS

*In the UK every year, solvent abuse
kills about 100 people:*
- *40% are first-time users*
- *the majority are aged between 14
and 17 years old.*

Tranquillizers were prescribed to
so many women they became
known as 'mother's little helpers'.

Legal drugs

Legal drugs are used widely and many people become addicted to them. Most have been an accepted part of our culture for hundreds of years.

Alcohol

Type of drug: **depressant**
Other names: drink, booze and many others
Legal status: anyone can drink alcohol at home; in **licensed premises** such as pubs and restaurants, under 14 year-olds cannot go into the bar; you have to be 18 to buy and drink alcohol in a bar; you have to be 18 to buy alcohol in supermarkets and other licensed shops

Alcohol is the most widely used and abused substance in human history. Alcoholic drinks such as beer and wine are made from fermented fruits, vegetables or grains. Spirits are further refined and distilled to make them stronger.

A little alcohol is said to be good for the heart, but too much too often can lead to addiction and diseases of the liver, heart and arteries. Alcohol can make you feel more confident and relaxed, but its depressant effects will eventually bring

you down and may cause emotional outbursts or aggression. Alcohol also affects co-ordination and judgement, which is why it is unsafe to drink and drive. A heavy drinking session often leads to a hangover the next morning. A hangover is caused by **dehydration** and too much alcohol in the blood.

Small children can get hooked on caffeine by drinking too much cola.

EFFECTS OF ALCOHOL ABUSE

- Alcohol is a factor in most violent assaults.

- In the majority of road accidents either the driver or victim is over the legal limit.

Caffeine

Type of drug: **stimulant**
Legal status: unrestricted

Caffeine is one of the most **addictive** and widely used legal stimulants in the world. It is found naturally in tea, coffee, cocoa, chocolate and is added to cola. Millions of people are dependent on caffeine without even being aware of it, but healthier **decaffeinated** drinks are becoming increasingly popular. Pure caffeine in its white crystal form is sometimes used to bulk out other drugs. Caffeine wakes you up and helps concentration, but too much can make you shaky. If you suddenly reduce a large caffeine intake then you may suffer withdrawal symptoms, usually in the form of bad headaches.

Tobacco

Type of drug: stimulant
Other names: **nicotine**, cigarettes, cigars, fags, smokes
Legal status: it is illegal to sell tobacco products to anyone under 16. Cigarette and tobacco packets and advertisements have to carry health warnings.

Before the health hazards were known, smoking was seen as a glamorous activity and was often advertised in association with a sporty, healthy, outdoor life. But nicotine is highly addictive and damaging to the health.

Smoking raises the pulse rate and blood pressure, yet it has a calming effect, reduces anxiety and stress, and suppresses the appetite. Continued smoking can cause lung or throat cancer, heart disease and bronchitis. A pregnant woman can harm her unborn child by smoking.

Smoking also harms any non-smokers who are forced to breathe polluted air in smoky places. Many employers in offices, airlines and restaurant chains are facing huge **compensation** claims from people who have become ill after continual exposure to smoke at work. Many smokers who have smoking-related diseases are also claiming compensation from tobacco companies, who for years deliberately concealed the health dangers.

Tobacco is the only product that harms people when used exactly as the manufacturer intended.

27

Drugs in sport

Athletes have used various substances to improve their performance for at least 2000 years. The winner of a sprint event in the Olympic Games as far back as 668 BC put his success down to dried figs!

There is more than a medal at stake. Successful athletes can earn millions from television appearances and sponsorship deals.

Using drugs – cheating and unethical?

Today most people think that using drugs in sport is both cheating and **unethical**. It also damages the reputation of individuals and sport as a whole.

Testing for drugs

Athletes were first tested for drugs at the 1968 Mexico Olympics. Every year, thousands of competitors in every sport are tested during training and at events. Some are found with traces of drugs in their blood or urine samples. Others are found to have tampered with their sample to prevent detection. Drug traces usually mean a ban lasting several years – long enough to ruin an athlete's chances of competing in the next Olympics.

What drugs do athletes use?

Different drugs are used by athletes for different effects. There are drugs that stimulate, keeping the athletes awake and confident during events. They may use anabolic steroids, or **hormone** growth drugs, that build muscle and increase strength. They may take pain killers to block local pain or injury, or **beta-blockers** to calm them down before competing. Others might use **blood-doping** to increase oxygen and improve muscle stamina.

Why athletes take the risk

Losing, coming second or reaching the line a split second after someone else is not good enough for an athlete who has been training for years to win. Drugs can give the athlete that extra edge. If other competitors are taking drugs, their only chance of winning might be to take them as well.

Other ways of winning

Beyond the training that develops their natural potential, athletes also try to get an advantage by using the best and most advanced equipment. Some receive better training because they have access to improved facilities. They may be sent overseas by sponsors to countries with better facilities. Most athletes also use food supplements that give a sudden boost of energy – and these are legal.

Should drugs be legalized in sport?

Some athletes and officials believe that because of these other ways in which athletes can gain advantages, competing will always be unequal. As a result, they say that performance-enhancing drugs might as well be allowed. The focus, they believe, should be shifted away from bans, public shaming and punishments to the development of safer ways of using the drugs, and to the education of athletes, so that they know the potential health risks.

RULES OF THE INTERNATIONAL OLYMPIC COMMITTEE

Many common medicines, such as remedies for coughs and colds, contain drugs banned by the International Olympic Committee. An athlete testing positive may be banned for **inadvertent** (unintentional) drug use..

Drugs in the media

Films and television bring many impressions about drugs into everyday life. They show how drugs are often associated with glamorous lifestyles, wealth and success, and how the police are engaged in an endless battle to keep drugs off the street and get drug **dealers** put behind bars. They reveal the miseries associated with drugs through **addicts** who subject themselves to every kind of shame for the next desperate fix. They depict rival gangs fighting it out on the streets and smugglers risking their freedom for the chance of big money.

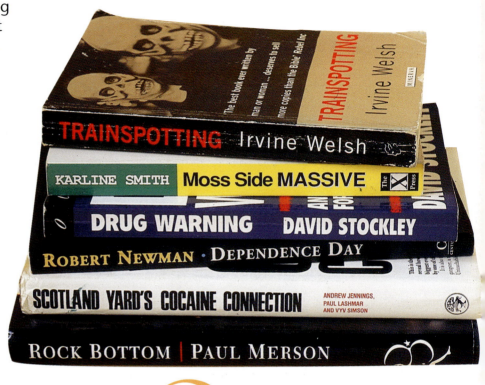

Drugs have always been good for business in the film and publishing worlds.

A new look at drugs

Young film-makers and writers are producing a new style of work that celebrates the culture and language of drug use. Some people view this as a dangerous influence, but others believe it is an important development in allowing true stories about drugs to be told. Because the ideas come from a youthful point of view, they communicate to other young people in an effective way. The drugs scene may look interesting, even irresistible, at first glance but when shown by people who have experienced it for real, it soon appears sordid and sad.

DRUGS AND THE MUSIC SCENE

Music and drugs have always been closely connected and rock stars have always been exposed for their drug use. But the dance drug, ecstasy, has probably had more songs written about it than any other – with the possible exception of alcohol. The coded references to drugs in pop songs reinforces the culture, excluding adults and others who are not in the 'know'.

Just one Ecstasy tablet took Leah Betts.

MAIDEN

This poster is part of an anti-drugs campaign. It shows Leah Betts who died after taking ecstasy on her eighteenth birthday. Tragic stories like this one make the news. An equally true story about a successful struggle against drugs would not.

The influence of the media

Stories in the press and television news paint a very one-sided picture of drug use. Big drug seizures, gang killings, a rise in heroin use, a sudden ecstasy death – all these make good headline news and sell the papers. No news editor is interested in the other side of the story. We do not get to read about the addict who manages to get off drugs once and for all, the person who is offered a chance to make money from drugs and says no, the family that faces destruction because of drugs but survives and grows closer through the experience. The media choose the most dramatic stories and in doing so influence the range of information available.

Documentaries

Unlike news and drama programmes, television documentaries tend to explore the culture of drugs more thoroughly. They look back over the history of drug use and its influence on creative lives. Drug use appears as a pattern of fads and trends. Both the fun elements and the cold reality of drug deaths and addictions are vividly depicted through the people who are actually involved. The misery of long-term addiction is never so convincing as when shown by someone desperately searching for a vein to inject.

The more honest and in-depth the documentary, the later at night it is likely to be shown. As a result, young people who are at the point of making decisions about drugs, are often excluded from the most powerful and reliable information available.

Dependence on drugs for a living

The media shows little interest in where drugs actually come from, even though the subject is an important part of the drugs story. There are people in the drug-producing countries whose livelihood, rarely from choice, depends on growing the cannabis plant, the opium poppy that makes heroin and the coca plant that makes cocaine and crack. These are not wealthy **drug barons** who profit from selling drugs to the developed world, but poor farmers who have little control over their own lives.

The men, women and even children who cultivate these crops rarely own their own land. Many are tied, through debt, to their employers or landlords. They have been offered loans over the years to help them meet basic needs, but can never earn enough to pay the loans off. Debt makes slaves of the workforce and keeps them obedient – often under threat of death.

Workers in drug-producing areas know their livelihood is insecure. The government, rival drug-growers or overseas drug enforcement agencies all have an interest in destroying the crop before it is harvested. Any worker suspected of alerting outsiders to the whereabouts of illegal crops is shot without question.

Workers in these opium poppy fields have no employment rights, no health or safety protection and receive no benefits if they become sick or too old to work.

Chemicals may help produce a good yield of cannabis, but it is the workers who pay the price with their health.

Dangerous farming methods

The use of pesticides and insecticides increases the output of these highly profitable crops. The landowners do not care if the chemicals used are toxic – they are not concerned about the health of their workers or those who will consume the drug. Powerful pesticides and insecticides can cause serious respiratory disease. Handling the chemicals and spraying the crops with them is dangerous as they can enter the body through the skin. Safety controls do not apply. Substances banned for use in the developed world are all too easily sent off to this ready market, or sold cheaply by western chemical wholesalers who know there will be no paperwork to link them to the buyer.

Destroying crops destroys lives

The governments of drug-producing countries often find it is wise to appear to co-operate with the governments of countries where drug use is a problem. For example, Columbia aims to co-operate with the US Drug Enforcement Agency. Even when officials of the producing country are taking generous bribes from the drug barons, it is politically useful to seem to show concern to the outside world. This may take the form of a sudden display of force, such as raids on certain drug-producing areas and the destruction of crops. Fields may be cut down or burnt, or herbicides such as powerful weed-killers may be sprayed from planes to kill the plants before harvest time. But it is likely to be the helpless workers who suffer most. They will not be paid if their crops are destroyed; they will not receive treatment if the herbicide makes them sick; and no one will care if there are birth defects in their community long after the crop spraying planes have gone.

Drug trafficking

Like anything else that is produced in one country and sold in another, drugs have to be moved from the country of origin to the end user. This illegal transportation is known as **trafficking**. Drugs, like other goods, tend to follow the traditional trade routes created by historical links with other countries. Police and customs officials co-operate worldwide to try and break up trafficking networks.

Easier trafficking

Before the early 1990s, there were strictly controlled borders between all the countries of Europe. Until 1989, the Berlin Wall was a further physical barrier between East and West. Britain and Eire, being islands, had their border controls at airports and seaports. Drug traffickers crossing Europe risked checks at every

Customs officers frequently use sniffer dogs to check suitcases for drugs. This has proved an effective means of identifying drug smugglers.

border and control point. Penetrating the Eastern block was even more difficult and dangerous. The situation changed in 1993 as the harmonization of Europe swept all those borders away.

Drug routes to the UK

The UK's historical trade links are with the Indian sub-continent, Europe, the Caribbean and parts of Africa. Cannabis sold in the UK comes mainly from North Africa, by boat or lorry. Heroin sold in the UK comes from southeast India, Pakistan, Afghanistan and Iran. It is shipped to Turkey and brought to the UK by lorry or boat. Cocaine sold in the UK comes from

South America, particularly Colombia, usually via Spain. Both Spain and Britain also have links with the Caribbean, and more cocaine comes in through these trade routes from Venezuela. Large quantities of cocaine are then exported from the UK to the rest of Europe.

Drug routes to the USA

The trading history of the USA involved the Far East and South America. Today, the heroin and some of the cannabis sold in North America comes from southeast Asia, Cambodia, Laos, Burma and Thailand. A great deal of cannabis for the home market is also illegally grown in the USA itself. Cocaine comes in directly from South America. The long-term trade links between North and South America have meant that America's cocaine (and more recently crack) problems are the worst in the world. Much of America's **black**

Drug trafficking follows the traditional routes established by trade and the colonization of other countries in the past.

market in drugs is controlled by the powerful families of the Sicilian Mafia.

Drug routes to Australia

Following Australia's traditional trade links, heroin and cannabis tend to come into the country from Thailand and northeast Asia, while ecstasy and cocaine are more likely to be shipped in from the UK.

From chemical store to dance floor

Ecstasy is a recent addition to the drug scene and has developed its own trafficking routes. Ecstasy is a totally **synthetic** substance made from raw chemicals. The bulk of these ingredients come from the industrial areas of northeastern Europe such as Poland, Latvia and Estonia. The breakdown of law and order in Eastern Europe created opportunities for the supply of drug-making chemicals to manufacturers throughout Europe. In the UK a heavy crackdown on ecstasy-producing laboratories soon pushed manufacture over to the Netherlands and Germany.

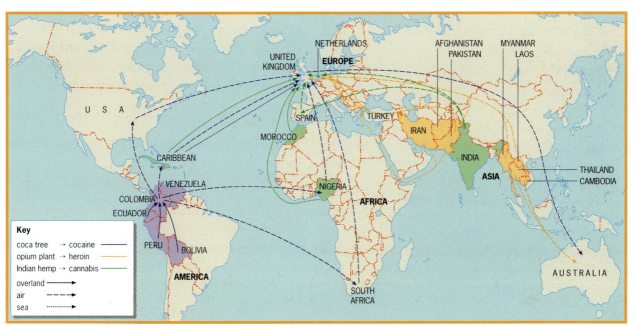

The war against drugs

The international effort to combat drug **trafficking** and crime is often called the war against drugs. This is not a real war but an endless struggle against large-scale criminal organizations and thousands of individuals who get rich selling drugs.

International co-operation

Police, drug enforcement agencies and customs officials worldwide co-operate by sharing information about drug-producing operations and the likely destinations of drug shipments.

Most large-scale production is controlled by powerful **drug barons** who avoid capture by letting others take the risks. These wealthy, ruthless barons often have their own well-equipped armies and stop at nothing to protect their interests.

Multiplying the profits

Beyond the drug barons a chain of **middlemen** are involved in transporting and distributing drugs to wholesalers, **dealers** and eventually the end user who buys drugs on the street. At each stage in the drug's journey the middlemen double their profits by bulking out, or **cutting**, the pure powders with similar looking substances. By the time the drugs reach the street they are only a fraction of their original purity.

Customs and Excise

Keeping drugs out of the country or seizing them as they come in is the task of Customs and Excise officers. As well as the random checks they carry out on lorries, boats, planes and their cargoes, they are involved in many long-planned operations that lead to massive drug hauls.

Letting others take the risk

Traffickers often hire people to take drugs into another country. The **courier**, sometimes called a **mule**, hides the drugs in their luggage, on their person or even inside their body. Sometimes people are tricked into carrying a package for someone else, unaware that it contains drugs. Drugs may be secretly hidden in their bags, to be retrieved by the owner once the unwitting courier has safely passed through customs. Every year thousands of paid couriers and people who have been tricked by traffickers are caught. Many try in vain to prove their innocence. In some countries the outcome can be life imprisonment or even execution.

INTERNATIONAL DRUG LAWS

Nearly all the countries in the world are members of the United Nations (UN) but there is little unity in their punishments for drug offences. Three out of four member countries have severe penalties such as life imprisonment, cutting off hands, or death. The UN is trying to persuade its members to adopt an agreed approach which recognizes a difference between **possession** and trafficking, and uses severe but more humane penalties.

FACT

In 1997–98, 13% of the UK total spending on drug-related issues was used in combating international supply.

Couriers often swallow lots of fragile drug-packed condoms. If one bursts in their stomach they are likely to die.

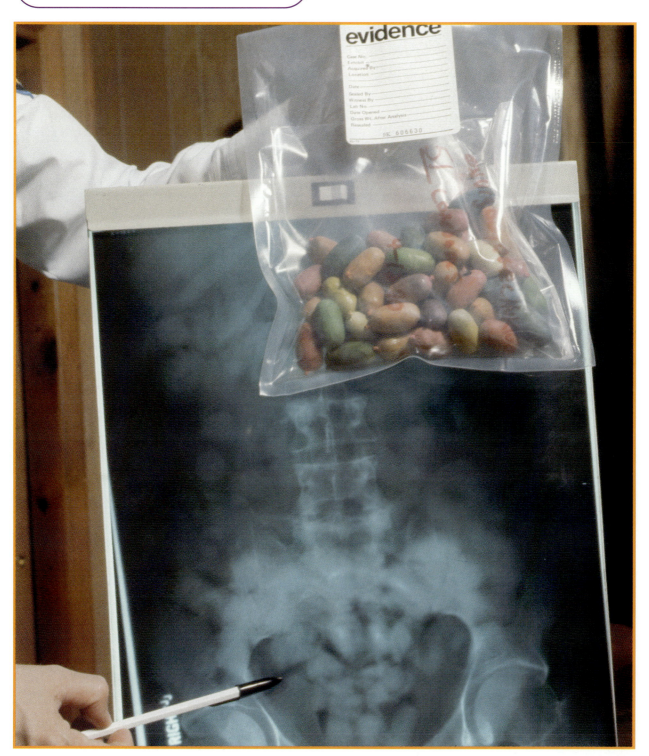

Drug prevention and education

Drug prevention is another part of the war against drugs. It describes a wide range of activities aimed at reducing or stopping drug use both locally and worldwide.

Government drug prevention strategies

Every government has its own approach to drug prevention. Government policies explain how drugs are policed and what sentences may be given to prevent or punish drug **trafficking**, dealing and **possession**. A government may also launch special campaigns to urge the public to contact the police if they have any information on drugs in their area.

Drug prevention campaigns

Information has to be got across to the public – to young people in particular. It needs to explain the legal and health dangers of using or abusing drugs. Over the past ten years, the approach has changed from expecting all young people to say no to drugs. It is now recognized that, without encouraging anyone to use drugs, you can still urge people who will use them to do so as safely as possible. This approach is known as **risk reduction** or **harm minimization**. It made public information about drugs much more accurate and honest.

Getting the message across

It is important that information reaches those who need it most. An acceptance that long-term drug users need information and help (rather than

FACTS

The UK Government's drug-related spending totalled 1.4 billion in 1997–98:
- *62% went on enforcement*
- *13% on treatment*
- *12% on prevention and education*
- *13% on combating international supply.*

Government drug prevention campaigns target groups of young people considered to be most at risk.

imprisonment or exclusion from society) has enabled very clear prevention and safety messages to be aimed at them. Local drug prevention workers build up trust with users in their area. They encourage users to seek help and run **needle exchanges** where people who inject drugs can get clean needles and so cut down the health risks of needle-sharing. People involved in crime or **prostitution** to fund their drug habits may receive support, health advice or counselling, and perhaps that vital chance to face the problems that lie behind their drug abuse.

Drug education in schools

Drug prevention and drug education are part of the curriculum in schools. The need for young people to be informed about the risks of drugs is now widely accepted, although some adults fear that by just mentioning drugs, ideas will be put into young people's heads.

Adults need drug education too

Educating parents and teachers is important too. Communication is often difficult because adults feel they do not know enough about drugs. Their reactions can seem extreme to young people, who may feel they need to protect their parents by not telling them drugs are around in their circle, or that friends are already experimenting. Even parents who have tried drugs themselves tend to focus on the dangers when it comes to their own children. Parents need to inform themselves and learn to talk about drugs in a calm, down-to-earth way if they want to develop a trusting dialogue with their children.

School drug policies

School drug policies are a useful way for pupils, parents, teachers and governors to know exactly where the school stands on drugs and drug use. The policy spells out what action will be taken if a student is found with drugs, tobacco or alcohol, whether the police will be involved and whether students may be suspended or permanently **excluded** if found dealing, taking or carrying drugs.

Young people learn the facts about drugs in school. Many parents attend similar evening or weekend sessions.

39

Drug legalization – conflicting issues

Many people, including some doctors, police chiefs and judges, believe that certain drugs should be **legalized**. They say that most of the ills associated with drugs and crime are caused by their illegal status. Cannabis is already **decriminalized** in the Netherlands and is openly sold in coffee shops.

People in favour of legalization see a number of advantages

- Drugs could be supplied to people who want them in pure, measured doses. The risk of unintentional overdose and the effects of toxic impurities would be lessened.
- People who choose to use drugs that are currently **controlled**, instead of tobacco or alcohol, would not face all the social disadvantages of fines, prison or a criminal record.
- Drug use would no longer have to be secret and sordid. It could become a social activity like drinking.
- Drugs would no longer be in the hands of organized criminals. The **black market** would die out.
- Gang warfare and murders associated with drug dealing would be a thing of the past. Drug products would be bought in shops.
- Customs, policing, court and prison costs would be massively reduced.
- Governments would be able to gather huge taxes on drugs, just as they already do on alcohol and tobacco.

Why are alcohol and tobacco legal?

The opposite side of the legalization argument asks why two of the most dangerous drugs in the world are legal.

Alcohol has serious health risks when abused. It is also highly **addictive**, the cause of the vast majority of road accidents, and a factor in almost all violent crimes and assaults. Every year tobacco kills more people than all other drugs put together. The cost of caring for people with smoking related diseases takes funds from other health needs. People who do not smoke are made ill, or even killed by the smoke from other people's tobacco. Unborn babies can be harmed in the womb by a smoking mother.

There is little doubt that if alcohol or tobacco were introduced today, they would become Class A **controlled drugs**. But historically they have been in free use for centuries. People who drink in moderation do not want to lose that freedom because of those who drink to excess. Smokers do not want to lose the right to damage their own health if they so choose.

If drugs were legalized, manufacturers would be quick to meet the demand in what would soon become a multimillion pound tax-paying market.

A UK national newspaper, *The Independent on Sunday*, ran a series of features which showed that thousands of people support the legalization of cannabis or think that it should be available for medical use.

governments spend increasing amounts of money on campaigns warning of the health risks. People argue that if no one smoked or drank, a country's medical costs would be reduced and so make up for any loss of taxes.

Taxes

The real reason alcohol and, particularly, tobacco remain legal is that governments earn a huge amount from them in tax revenue. Without that income unpopular cuts would have to be made in spending money on welfare, health, education and policing. Alternatively, direct taxes would have to be increased, but people do not want to pay more tax from their wage packets and so may not support a government that increases taxation. As long as tobacco and alcohol earn their keep, no government can afford to totally ban their use. However, some

What can you do about drugs?

Drugs are part of our society and, at some time or another, most young people find themselves faced with choices about whether to try drugs or not. This is as likely for smoking tobacco and drinking alcohol as it is for trying **controlled drugs**, although of course the legal risks are different.

If asked, most young people around the age of 11 say they have no intention of trying drugs. They are aware of the dangers and feel drug users are stupid. But as they get older, drugs sometimes seem more attractive, opportunities to experiment may come along and friends may put pressure on to give drugs a try.

It is then that the question of whether to smoke, drink alcohol or try controlled drugs becomes a personal issue. The more informed and intelligent you are about drugs, the less likely you are to be influenced by others.

1 INFORM YOURSELF

Read about drugs – a fiction and non-fiction list is supplied on page 47 and there are books on drugs, alcohol and smoking in your school or public library. The library will also have addresses of local drug information agencies in your area which may have their own leaflets and magazines.

2 FIND OUT ABOUT YOUR SCHOOL'S DRUG POLICY

Check it is on display where everyone can see it.

3 CONTACT YOUR SCHOOL LIAISON OFFICER

Ask your teacher to contact the local School Liaison Officer via the police station. They will have detailed knowledge about the drug problems in your area and have plenty of information about drugs and the law.

4 VISIT A POLICE STATION

Ask your teacher to help you arrange a visit to a police station to see exactly what happens when someone is arrested. It can be quite an eye-opener to discover how much information is gathered about a person who gets into trouble with the police and what happens to them.

5 GET INVOLVED IN PEER EDUCATION

Become a **counsellor** or drug adviser for your school. Make it your business to find out the facts. Get your school on the mailing list for locally produced information.

There are plenty of ways to have fun and enjoy life without getting involved with drugs!

6 INFORM YOUR FRIENDS

Organize drug information days at your school. You could prepare fact sheets on different drugs, or concentrate on a particular drug in your area.

7 DEBATE THE ISSUE

Talk to your friends and family in an open and honest way. Don't be afraid to tell your parents if drugs are around or on offer – they will be glad to know you are taking a responsible attitude.

8 MAKE YOUR OWN CHOICES

Think twice, then think again, before even considering trying drugs, cigarettes or alcohol. It's your life, so never do it to please or impress someone else. Whatever choices you make, make them your own, and make them informed.

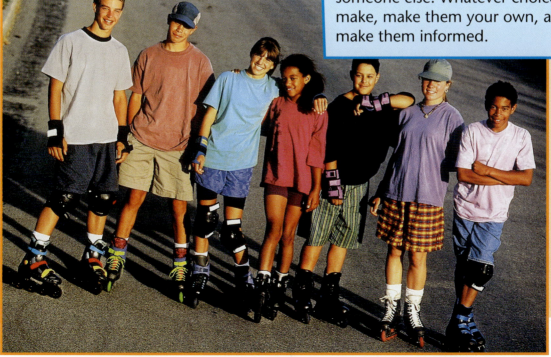

Glossary

abscess infected pus-filled wound

addict someone who cannot give something up

addictive habit forming; compelling

adrenaline stimulating **hormone** from the adrenal gland

AIDS Acquired Immune Deficiency Syndrome – illnesses that develop from **HIV** infection

allergy abnormal reaction or sensitivity

altered perception changed way of seeing things

anaesthetic substance that numbs or kills pain

beta-blocker drug that reduces heart rate and stress

black market illegal trade in goods

blood-doping injecting more blood into the body to increase oxygen and improve stamina

caution (legal) a warning that can be given for certain offences instead of taking someone to court

compensation payment to make up for loss or injury

controlled drugs drugs whose use or possession is governed by certain laws

courier (drugs) person who carries drugs on behalf of another

cut bulk out drugs by diluting them with similar substances

dealer person who supplies drugs

decaffeinated with the caffeine removed

decriminalize make something no longer a criminal offence

dehydrate dry out; lose liquid to a dangerous extent

depressant drug that sedates or lowers activity

drug baron powerful person who controls drug production and supply

exclude (school) shut out, prevent from attending

fermentation organic breakdown of material that creates alcohol

gangrene death and decay of flesh

hallucinate see or imagine things that are not real

hallucinogen substance causing people to see or imagine things

hallucinogenic causing people to see and imagine things

hangover unpleasant after-effect of too much alcohol

harm minimization ways of lessening the risks of potentially harmful activities

HIV Human Immunodeficiency Virus – a virus attacking the immune system

hepatitis disease of the liver

high feeling good on drugs

hormone natural body secretion that has physical effects

hypodermic under the skin; a needle for injecting

inadvertent unintentional

infertility inability to have children

intoxicate make drunk or high

laudanum drug made from opium

legalize make legal

licensed premises places permitted to sell alcohol under license

middlemen people in the middle of a trading or communication chain

mind-altering changing how one sees or imagines things

morphine drug made from opium

mule person who carries drugs on behalf of others

narcotic pain-killer, sleep-inducing drug

needle exchange place where drug injectors can swap used needles for safe, clean ones

nicotine active ingredient in tobacco

opiate any drug containing opium

over-the-counter things that can be bought freely in a shop

paranoia mental condition, involving fears and imaginings

perception the way things are seen or understood

possession (drugs) offence of having or being responsible for a drug

prescribed issued under the direction of a doctor

probation legal supervision instead of prison

prosecute charge and take to court

prostitution selling sex for money

psychological relating to the mind or thoughts

Rastafarian West Indian religious and political sect

risk reduction reduce risk to a safer level

ritual religious or cultural ceremony

rush sudden and intense, short-lived feeling

septicaemia infection of the blood

sexual abuse harmful sexual treatment

solvents substances that have vapours, such as glues and gases

stimulant something that wakes one up or gives energy

substance abuse harmful use of a substance

suffocation death through lack of oxygen

synthetic artificial, made by people

testosterone natural male **hormone**

trafficking transport and distribution of drugs

tranquillizer drug that calms or puts to sleep

trip vision-filled journey-like experience that people on hallucinogenic drugs may have

unethical morally wrong

volatile evaporating, giving off vapour

Contacts and helplines

ADFAM (Advice for Families of Drug Users)

Waterbridge House
32–36 Loman Street, London, SE1 OEE
0171 928 8900
Information about alcohol abuse

ASH (Action for Smoking and Health)

109 Gloucester Place, London, W1H 3PH
0171 935 6120
Web site: http://www.ash.org
Anti-smoking organization

DRUGS IN SCHOOL

0345 366666
Free helpline offering drugs advice

HEALTH EDUCATION AUTHORITY

(look in a telephone directory for your local authority)

ISDD (Institute for the Study of Drug Dependence)

Waterbridge House, 32–36 Loman Street
London, SE1 OEE
0171 928 1211
Web site: http://www.isdd.co.uk
Research library and resources

LIFELINE

101-103 Oldham Street
Manchester, M4 1LW
0161 839 2054
Advice and information

NATIONAL DRUGS HELPLINE

0800 776600
24-hour free drugs advice

PARENTLINE (Formerly OPUS)

Rayfa House, 57 Hart Road, Thunderley
Essex, SS7 3PD
01268 757077
Advice for parents of drug abusers

RELEASE

388 Old Street, London, EC1V 9LT
0171 729 9904
Legal and drug information advice

RE-SOLV

30a High Street, Stone
Staffordshire, ST15 8AW
01785 817885
Information about volatile substance abuse

In Australia use the following contacts:

AUSTRALIAN DRUG FOUNDATION

Web site: http://www.adf.org.au
Information and contacts

CEIDA (Centre for Education on Information on Drugs and Alcohol)

Web site: http://www.ceida.net.au
Information and contacts

NATIONAL CAMPAIGN AGAINST DRUG ABUSE

(02) 6289 8654 – Advice and information

NATIONAL DRUG AND ALCOHOL RESEARCH CENTRE

Baker Street, Randwick, NSW 2031
Australia
(02) 9398 9333
Research library and resources

Further reading

Fiction

The Ups and Downs of Carl Davis the Third
A novel in letter form
Collins Educational, 1994

Jacqueline Hyde
Robert Swindells
Doubleday, 1996

Junk
Melvyn Burgess
Penguin, 1996

Run Donny Run!
Joe Buckley
Wolfhound Press, 1991

Tina Come Home
Paul Geraghty
Red Fox, 1994

Out Of It
Maureen Stewart
Puffin, 1995

Orfe
Cynthia Voight
Harper Collins, 1993

Non-fiction

Alcohol
Iris Webb
Wayland, Points of View series, 1991

D-Brief – The Truth About Drugs (magazine for teenagers)

D-Word – Let's Talk About Drugs (magazine for parents)
Institute for the Study of Drug Dependence, 1998

D-Code (drug information CD Rom)
Health Education Authority

Dealing with Drug Abuse
Yvette Soloman and John Colman
Wayland *Dealing with… series*, 1995

Drug Trafficking
Jillian Powell
Watts Books, Crimebusters series, 1996

Drugs and Crime
Marcella Foster and Joe Sheehan
Wayland, 1992

Drugs and Medicine
Jenny Bryan
Wayland, 1992

Drugs and Sport
Christian Wolmar
Wayland, 1992

Right to Smoke?
Emma Haughton
Watts Books, *Viewpoints* series, 1996

The House That Crack Built
Clark Taylor
Chronicle, 1994

The Party's Over: Living without Leah
Janet & Paul Betts with Ivan Sage
Robson Books, 1997

We're Talking About Drugs
Jenny Bryan
Wayland, 1995

What Do You Know About Drinking Alcohol?
Pete Sanders and Steve Myers
Watts Books, 1989

Index